Mostly Metals

A Beginner's Guide to Jewelry Design

Mostly Metals

A Beginner's Guide to Jewelry Design

Karin Buckingham

Kalmbach Publishing, Waukesha, Wis.

Contents

Printed in the United States of America

12 11 10 09 08   1 2 3 4 5

Distributed to the trade by Watson-Guptill

Visit our Web site at
www.BeadAndCraftBooks.com
Secure online ordering available

Publisher's Cataloging-in-Publication Data
Buckingham, Karin.
  Mostly metals : a beginner's guide to jewelry design / Karin Buckingham.
    p. : col. ill. ; cm.
  ISBN: 978-0-87116-259-5
1. Jewelry making–Handbooks, manuals, etc.
2. Metal-work–Handbooks, manuals, etc.
I. Title.

TT212 .B83 2008
739.27

Introduction

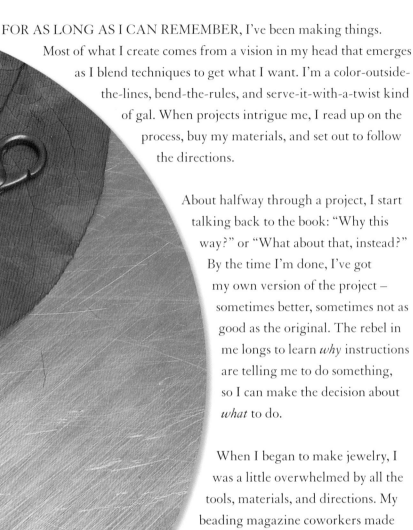

FOR AS LONG AS I CAN REMEMBER, I've been making things. Most of what I create comes from a vision in my head that emerges as I blend techniques to get what I want. I'm a color-outside-the-lines, bend-the-rules, and serve-it-with-a-twist kind of gal. When projects intrigue me, I read up on the process, buy my materials, and set out to follow the directions.

About halfway through a project, I start talking back to the book: "Why this way?" or "What about that, instead?" By the time I'm done, I've got my own version of the project – sometimes better, sometimes not as good as the original. The rebel in me longs to learn *why* instructions are telling me to do something, so I can make the decision about *what* to do.

When I began to make jewelry, I was a little overwhelmed by all the tools, materials, and directions. My beading magazine coworkers made gentle suggestions: "Make sure your loops are round!" "Watch your ends!" "Don't use a wrapped loop there; it should be a plain loop!"

Little decisions made along the way have a lot to do with creating beautiful designs.

I kept asking *why*. Slowly but surely, things started to fall into place. I began to understand the reasoning behind the directions and how the little decisions made along the way have a lot to do with creating beautiful designs.

Conjure your inner artiste

Mostly Metals begins with easy skills and builds as it goes along. I think that's the best way to learn. Skip around if you'd like, but if you're a true first-timer, you'll find it easier to begin at the beginning. Practice the techniques in order to master them. But more than techniques, I hope to teach you some of the logic behind good design – what works, when, and why – to help you make informed choices as you begin to create your original, fabulous jewelry.

Some people believe you need to be granted the title of artist or designer from admiring fans. I believe if you have a curious mind, a creative spirit, a love for things unique, and a mastery of the skills involved, you *are* a designer.

Why metal?

I've always been drawn to the clean lines and strong shapes of precious metal jewelry. When I was young, I collected silver bangle bracelets, tiny hammered rings, and dangling earrings from arts & crafts fairs my family would visit during our summer vacations. As lovely as these pieces were, now I know they were simply well-executed examples of some of the most elementary jewelry-making techniques. Today I could make them myself – and that's a great feeling.

I believe it's OK to begin with good-quality purchased components such as head pins, jump rings, and chain (see pages 10–12). Many jewelry artists make their own components, but that requires a little more equipment than I call for here. For the projects in this book, you won't need a torch or solder and you can leave the pickle in the jar. You can make all of my jewelry projects with two pairs of pliers and a wire cutter. The guide on pages 13–14 explains which tools you *must* have and shows a few extras that are nice to have.

You can make all of my jewelry projects with two pairs of pliers and a wire cutter.

You'll see plenty of gemstones and crystals sprinkled throughout these pages, but in each project, metal is the key design component. Metal components open doors to designs you just can't accomplish with bead-stringing alone.

For example, chain is a great problem solver: I love working with leather cord, but I had a hard time finding silver beads with holes large enough to string on the cord. The necklace on page 60 was born from this challenge, and I couldn't be happier with the outcome.

The donuts that found their way into the necklace on page 68 were a similar challenge. I adored them when I bought them, but what to do with them? Suspending them from fine chain was my solution, and I love the elegant drape it provides.

It's fun to wear jewelry you've made, knowing it could pass for store-bought jewelry. The right combination of bright, shiny components and quality workmanship brings it all together.

Materials and tools

This overview covers most of the basic materials and tools you'll see when you begin to shop for jewelry-making supplies. The selection can be overwhelming, so use this visual guide to identify what you need for the project at hand. Selecting tools will be simpler; most of the projects in this book use only the "top three" tools: roundnose pliers, chainnose pliers, and diagonal wire cutters. As your skills progress and you become more committed to your jewelry making, you may decide to acquire some of the other tools shown.

Materials

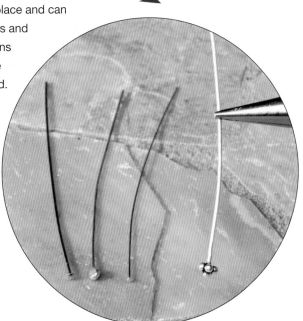

Head pins hold beads in place and can be used for embellishments and connections. Plain head pins resemble a nail; decorative head pins have a fancy end. Lengths of 1 to 3 inches are common, and head pins come in several gauges (thicknesses) of wire. If the hole in your bead is too large for the end of the headpin, just string a seed bead or spacer first, and you'll be all set.

Eye pins have a loop at the end that holds the bead in place, can be linked to another loop, or acts as a decorative embellishment. After you learn how to make a plain loop in Chapter 1, you can make your own eye pins. If you're making a project with lots of links, such as the earrings on page 21, eye pins can be a time-saver, but I usually just turn my own loops from wire.

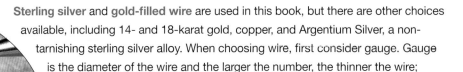

Sterling silver and **gold-filled wire** are used in this book, but there are other choices available, including 14- and 18-karat gold, copper, and Argentium Silver, a non-tarnishing sterling silver alloy. When choosing wire, first consider gauge. Gauge is the diameter of the wire and the larger the number, the thinner the wire; 22-gauge is a good working wire; 26-gauge is thin enough to go through small holes, such as those in pearls; 16-gauge is quite thick and is better for sturdier projects like bracelets. Next, consider hardness. As you work with wire, the molecules in the metal are rearranged and the wire becomes firmer, or work-hardened. In some ways, this is good – the wire will hold the shape you are creating. But if you overwork metal, it becomes brittle and breakable. For the best results with the projects in this book, use wire that is half-hard, or tempered.

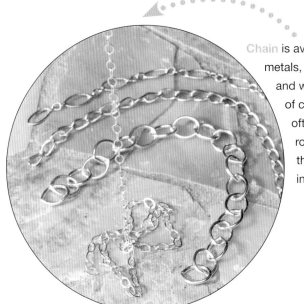

Chain is available in a variety of metals, sizes, styles, textures, and weights – you'll have a lot of choices to make! Most often, chain is sold off a roll, and you can purchase the exact length called for in a project.

Split rings are like tiny key rings. The spiral of wire keeps whatever you've attached – a link of chain, a dangle with a loop, a manufactured charm – in place. Use them when you need a secure connection or at the end of a strung necklace (the beading wire can't slide through, like it can with a plain jump ring).

Jump rings are connectors, but as you'll see in Chapter Three, they can drive the design of your jewelry. Choose well-made, sturdy jump rings that will hold their shape. Thicker gauges work when the jump rings are part of the design.

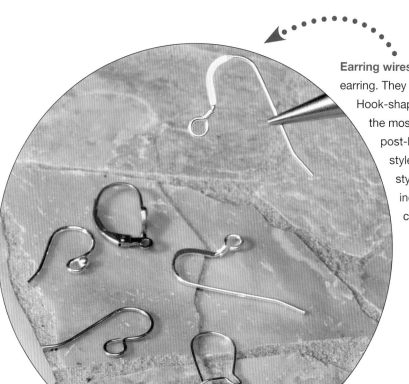

Earring wires turn your dangle into an earring. They are available in many styles. Hook-shaped and lever-back wires are the most popular. You also can buy post-back, screw-back, and hoop styles. Many of the hook-shaped styles have extra embellishments, including beads, springs, charms, or gemstones.

Clasps are as important to your design as any other element. You want a functional clasp but you also want to consider one that balances the weight of your piece, complements your design, is pretty to look at, and is easy to use. *Toggle clasps,* also called bar-and-loop clasps, work with the tension of the bracelet or necklace to stay closed. Sometimes it's hard to maneuver the bar end – simply string a few extra round spacer beads on that side and you'll be pleased with the added flexibility. *Spring clasps* are round "trigger" clasps and hook to a jump ring or a link of chain. *Lobster claw clasps* are similar to spring clasps in construction, but the shape resembles a lobster's claw. *S-clasps* and *hook clasps* hook into a large ring. *Box clasps* are elegant, and often have several loops so they are ideal for multistrand bracelets. *Slide clasps* also provide a secure and attractive connection for multistrand jewelry.

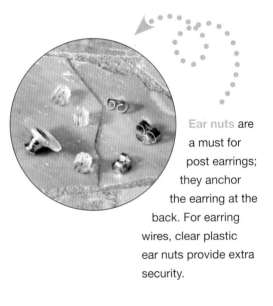

Ear nuts are a must for post earrings; they anchor the earring at the back. For earring wires, clear plastic ear nuts provide extra security.

Crimp tubes, sometimes called crimp beads, are the finishing security for any project strung on flexible beading wire. I prefer sterling silver 1 x 2mm crimp tubes. They flatten into a nice square or fold easily for a slim profile.

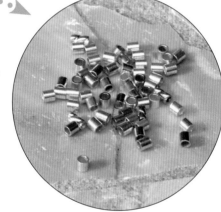

Precious metals are just that – pure and rare. Sterling silver and 14-karat gold are the most common. Base metals are not precious and therefore are much less expensive. Plated metals are base metals that have been coated with a precious metal. "Gold filled" refers to material (often brass) to which a layer of gold has been fused.

Tools

Must-have pliers

Roundnose pliers have round, tapered jaws and are used most often to form loops. Control the size of loops by the adjusting the position of the wire on the pliers' jaw.

Chainnose pliers have smooth, flat, tapered jaws. They are great for getting into tight spots, such as when you need to grasp a tiny length of wire to finish a wrapped loop. Use chainnose pliers to flatten a crimp bead. They also are ideal for opening and closing jump rings, as the smooth jaw provides a tight grasp on the metal. Start with one pair, but if you are doing a lot of work with jump rings, you may want a second pair.

Nice-to-have pliers

The tiny hook at the tip of **split ring pliers** wedges open the coils of a split ring so you can easily attach a charm or dangle.

Bentnose pliers have uses similar to chainnose pliers, but the bent tips make it even easier to grasp wire in tight spaces.

Crimping pliers are used with crimp tubes in a two-step process that creates folded crimps. Folded crimps are a secure, professional-looking finish for strung jewelry; they are small and can be hidden inside a large-hole bead. (If you don't have crimping pliers, you can make a flattened crimp with chainnose pliers.)

Extras

Nylon-jaw pliers won't nick or dent wire as you work. They also work well for straightening wire. They are especially useful for wireworkers.

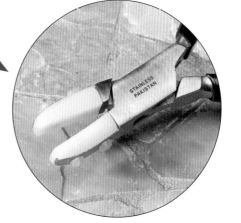

Must-have cutters

Diagonal wire cutters cut wire and beading wire with a nice, diagonal edge which is perfect for finishing wrapped loops. Most diagonal wire cutters have a back edge that cuts flush, which is desirable after crimping or for wire ends.

Nice-to-have cutters

Heavy-duty wire cutters are best for base metals that can be harder and may nick your diagonal wire cutters. Heavy duty wire cutters are a must for cutting memory wire.

Extras

Calipers measure the size of a bead in both millimeters and inches. When you're in a creative mood, you can bead whatever looks good together without worrying what size the beads are. But if you're following a pattern or you spill your stash, you may need help to tell the 2mms from the 3mms. Calipers also are useful for measuring beads you'd like to replace, so you can be sure to buy the same size.

Flexible beading needles have a large eye that's easy to thread, but it completely collapses as it's drawn through the bead, so you can string pearls or other small-hole beads with ease. Beading needles are most often used with ribbon elastic.

A **clamp** is a lifesaver for any stringing project. You can use a small binder clip or a patented product called a Bead Stopper. I like the Bead Stopper; you simply grip the end of the beading wire in the spring, and the beads won't go flying off the end. Each clip can hold several wires, so it works for multistrand projects as well.

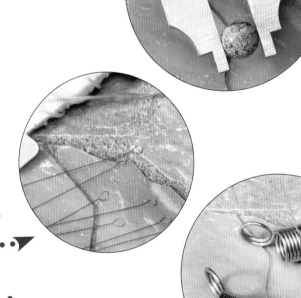

Jewelry-making workspace

Where do you work? I have a fabulous studio that streams with sunlight. My well-organized shelves keep all my beads at my fingertips, and I'm free to design all day long. Well, in my fantasies, I do. The truth is that I make all my jewelry at my dining room table (although I do get some nice sunlight). Realities, like dogs and cats (sometimes misbehaving), telephones, car pools, forgot-my-lunch emergencies, the need for dinner to be made, and the rest of life means even on a day dedicated to beading, I'm up and down a lot. And, because we eat a family dinner at the dining room table (aka my studio) every night, I need to be able to clean up quickly. I'd love the luxury of my own space, and for now I can dream about it. My compromise is a set of extra-large stacking trays. I have one for gemstones and pearls, one for seed beads, one for crystals, and one for silver and gold. When I'm in designing mode, I can spread them out and see what I have at a glance. When it's time to clean up, they stack vertically and get tucked away on a shelf.

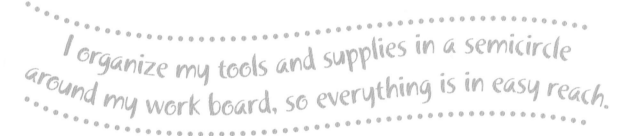

I organize my tools and supplies in a semicircle around my work board, so everything is in easy reach.

I also have a work board that I made out of a piece of plywood covered with quilter's batting and Ultrasuede. Because it's stiff, I can carry a work in progress back and forth without putting every little element away. The Ultrasuede keeps my beads from rolling around, and the batting provides a little "give" so I can pick up beads with a wire right from the surface. I tend to organize my tools and supplies in a semicircle around my work board, so everything is in easy reach. Oh, and because I'm the type to have several projects going at once, I have a few baking sheets lined with dish towels for my never-enough-time-to-finish projects. These are easy to keep stacked until the muse strikes, and then I pull out the project and make a little more progress. Just don't ask me for a bake-sale donation!

You might start with a series of plastic containers (I did). As you build your bead stash, you'll find new ways to organize things. Is it important that you sort by color or type of material? Your needs will drive your solution, and it will be unique to you.

Chapter One
Designing with the plain loop

How to make a plain loop

1. String a bead on a head pin, trim the end of the wire to ⅜ in. (1cm), and bend it at a right angle over the bead. (To make a plain loop at the end of a wire with no bead, grasp the wire with chainnose pliers ⅜ in. from the end and make a right-angle bend.)

2. Grasp the end of the wire with your roundnose pliers about ⅛ in. (3mm) from the tip of the jaw. Use your index finger to check that the wire end is flush with the edge of the pliers. If you feel a stub of wire, you've grasped too far away from the end, so adjust your pliers. Gently roll the wire until you can't roll comfortably anymore.

3. Reposition the pliers and continue to roll the loop. The tip of the wire should meet your initial bend, and you should have a perfect, centered wire circle.

TIP If your wire is too long, continue rolling past the initial bend until you have a perfect circle. Trim the excess tail with the tip of your diagonal wire cutters.

TIP Mark a piece of scrap wire at ⅜ in. (1cm) with a permanent marker and use it as a ruler when you trim the wire in step 1. Or, find a 10mm bead, which is exactly ⅜ in. long. Place the bead on the wire, trim the end flush, and remove the bead.

How to open and close a plain loop

Grasp the loop with two pairs of pliers held parallel to each other. Gently open the loop by moving one set of pliers forward and the other set backward.

Repeat the process in reverse to close the loop. Resist the temptation to unroll the loop – this will overwork the wire and weaken it, and you'll never get a perfectly round loop the second time.

For a quick refresher, refer to the review of basic techniques that starts on page 89 when you see an instruction that looks like this:

Open a jump ring

TIP

Plain loop earrings

Let's begin with some simple earrings.

a

b

c

1. String a crystal on a head pin. Trim the wire ⅜ in. (1cm) above the bead **(a)**.

2. Grasp the wire with the roundnose pliers and **make a plain loop (b)** to create a dangle. Repeat with the second crystal. Wrap at the same point on the pliers so the loops are exactly the same size.

3. Open the loop on an earring wire, add the dangle, and close the loop **(c)**. Repeat with the second earring wire and the second dangle. You've made your first pair of earrings!

For these pretty earrings, you'll need two 8mm bicone crystals, two 1½-in. (3.8cm) decorative head pins, and a pair of earring wires.

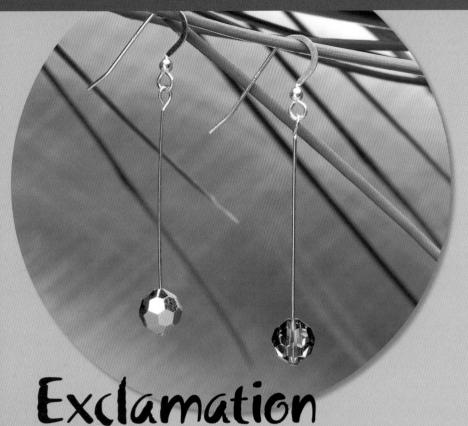

Exclamation point earrings

We'll do the same thing as we did in the first project, with the same beads, the same earring wires, and the same head pins. But instead of trimming the head pins, work ⅜ in. (1cm) away from the end of the long head pin.

a

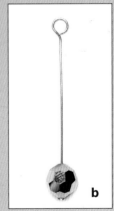

b

YOU NEED

- 2 8mm round crystals
- 2 2-in. (5cm) 22-gauge head pins, silver
- Pair of earring wires
- Roundnose pliers
- Chainnose pliers
- Diagonal wire cutters

1. Repeat steps 1–3 of **How to make a plain loop** on page 18 **(a, b)**. Look at the dramatic results – like an exclamation point! Make a second, add some earring wires, and you're done.

Link earrings

Once you've mastered plain loops, use them to connect beads into light, airy earrings. The most important thing to remember is to make your loops as round and as uniform as you can. This will keep your earrings the same length, and it just looks nicer, too!

a

1. String a 6mm bead onto a head pin and **make a plain loop** above the bead **(a)**.

- 4 6mm round beads, flake quartz
- 2 5mm round beads, garnet
- 2 1-in. (2.5cm) 22-gauge head pins
- 12 in. (30cm) 22-gauge wire, silver
- Pair of earring wires
- Roundnose pliers
- Chainnose pliers
- Diagonal wire cutters

YOU NEED

b

2. Make a plain loop at one end of a 3-in. (7.6cm) length of wire **(b)**. String a 5mm bead above the loop, and make a second plain loop above the bead. Repeat using a 6mm bead.

c

3. Open the bottom loop of the 5mm bead unit from step 2 and string the unit from step 1. Close the loop. Open the upper loop and add the 6mm unit from step 2 **(c)**. Close the loop.

d

4. Open the loop of an earring wire and attach the dangle **(d)**. Make a second earring to match the first.

Mark your roundnose pliers with a permanent marker about ⅛ in. (3mm) from the tip. Always work at this point and your loops will be the same size.

TIP

Cluster earrings

If one plain loop is fun, how about ten? Let's combine the elements of the last two projects into a pair of cluster earrings.

- 2 6mm round beads, gold filled
- 10 2mm round beads, silver
- 10 1-in. (2.5cm) 22-gauge head pins, silver
- 4 in. (10cm) 22-gauge wire, silver
- Pair of earring wires
- Roundnose pliers
- Chainnose pliers
- Diagonal wire cutters

YOU NEED

a

1. String a 2mm round bead on a head pin, and **make a plain loop** above the bead. Work at the tips of your roundnose pliers to create small loops. Repeat to make 10 bead units **(a)**.

b

2. Make a plain loop at the end of a 2-in. (5cm) length of wire. String a 5mm bead, and make a second plain loop above the bead. Work a little farther down the jaws of your pliers than you did in step 1 to get a larger loop. Repeat to make a second bead unit **(b)**.

c

3. Open one of the larger loops on a bead unit, string five dangles from step 1, and close the loop. Repeat with the second bead unit from step 2 and the remaining five dangles from step 1 **(c)**.

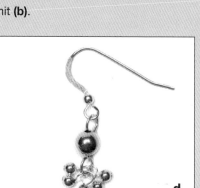

d

4. Open the loop of an earring wire, string the beaded unit onto the wire, and close the loop. Repeat to finish the second earring **(d)**.

Dangle pendant

A plain loop is a nice embellishment for a simple dangle, and is especially helpful if you don't have any head pins on hand.

- 8–12mm gemstone nugget
- 3 in. (7.6cm) 22-gauge wire, silver
- 15 in. (38cm) 2mm diameter leather cord
- 2 fold-over crimp ends
- 2 5mm jump rings
- Lobster claw clasp
- Roundnose pliers
- Chainnose pliers
- Diagonal wire cutters
- GS-Hypo Cement

YOU NEED

1. Make a plain loop at the end of a wire **(a)**, add a bead or two, and make another plain loop above the bead, perpendicular to the lower loop.

2. String the pendant on the cord for a simple necklace **(b)**. **Attach a fold-over crimp** to each cord end. Open the jump rings, add a lobster claw clasp to one, and attach a jump ring to each of the crimps. Close the jump rings.

a

b

Make the hanging (top) loop perpendicular to the bottom loop so the bottom loop shows as you wear the pendant. To do this, make the top bend to the right or left and make the bottom bend to the front or the back.

TIP

Vertical connector

One of my dad's favorite lines when I was growing up was "please be useful as well as decorative." While I am sure he was referring to clearing the table or doing the dishes, the plain loop is just that: useful and decorative.

This necklace is made from a few lengths of chain connected by a double-sided plain loop, proving its utility. The two-strand version, held with the same loop turned 90°, is featured on page 26.

1. Cut four two-link segments, one five-link segment, and two ten-link segments of chain **(a)**. (I'm using figure-eight chain here and counting the "8" as one segment.)

2. Cut a 1½-in. (3.8cm) length of wire (or trim the head from a 1½-in. head pin). Make a beaded unit by **making a plain loop** at one end, stringing a bead, and making a plain loop at the other end. Repeat to make a second beaded unit. Cut a 3-in.

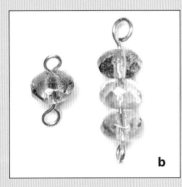

(7.6cm) length of wire. Make a beaded unit by making a plain loop at one end, stringing three beads, and making a plain loop at the other end. Repeat to make four units **(b)**.

3. Open one loop on a three-bead unit and connect it to the five-link segment of chain. Close the loop. Attach a three-bead unit to the other end of the five-link segment **(c)**.

4. Add a two-link segment, a one-bead unit, and a two-link segment. Add a three-bead unit and a ten-link segment **(d)**. Repeat on the other side.

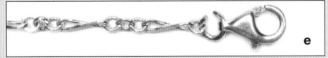

5. Open a jump ring, string the last link of chain and a lobster claw clasp, and close the jump ring **(e)**. Attach a jump ring to the other end link of chain.

- 14 6 x 4mm glass rondelles
- 15 in. (38cm) 22-gauge wire, silver
- 17 in. (43cm) figure-eight long-and-short chain, silver
- 2 5mm jump rings
- Lobster claw clasp
- Roundnose pliers
- Chainnose pliers
- Diagonal wire cutters

YOU NEED

Horizontal connector

- 16 6 x 4mm glass rondelles
- 8 3mm spacer beads, copper
- 16 in. (41cm) 22-gauge wire, copper
- 4 ft. (1.2m) curb chain, antique copper
- 3 5mm jump rings, copper
- Lobster claw clasp, antique copper
- Roundnose pliers
- Chainnose pliers
- Diagonal wire cutters

a

b

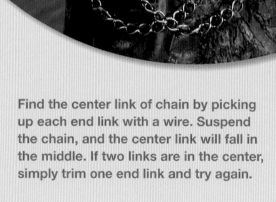

1. Cut a 2-in. (5cm) segment of wire (or trim the head from a 2-in. head pin). **Make a plain loop** at one end, string a bead, a spacer, and a bead, and make a plain loop at the other end **(a)**. Repeat to make eight beaded units.

2. Determine the finished length of your necklace. Subtract the clasp measurement and cut two pieces of chain to that length. This necklace is 24 in. (61cm) long. Find the center link of each chain. **Open the loop** on a beaded unit, attach the center length, and close the loop. Repeat with the other loop and the second piece of chain **(b)**.

Find the center link of chain by picking up each end link with a wire. Suspend the chain, and the center link will fall in the middle. If two links are in the center, simply trim one end link and try again.

TIP

c

d

e

3. Continue adding beaded units on each side, skipping 15 links between units **(c)**.

Plain loops are pretty, but they can pull apart if your jewelry snags on something. Use plain loops for connections in lightweight jewelry that won't be under a lot of stress, such as earrings or necklaces.

4. **Open a jump ring,** string the two end links of chain on one side, and close the jump ring. Repeat on the other side **(d)**.

5. Open a jump ring, string a lobster claw clasp and one end jump ring, and close the jump ring **(e)**.

TIP

Corkscrew earrings

These earrings are easy to make and fun to wear. You can use a chopstick, a wood skewer, or just about any narrow cylinder to shape the coils.

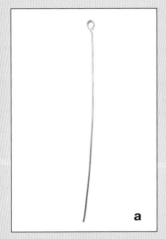

a

b

c

d

1. Cut a 6-in. (15cm) length of 18-gauge wire, and **make a plain loop** at one end **(a)**.

2. Coil the wire around a pencil **(b)**.

3. With chainnose pliers, bend the loop upright **(c)**.

4. Open the loop of an earring wire and connect the corkscrew. Close the loop **(d)**. Repeat to make a second earring. File the cut ends of the wire, if desired.

DESIGN IDEAS: Use 22- or 24-gauge wire and see how different a finer gauge makes the earrings look. For fun, make a few pairs with colored craft wire.

- 1 ft. (30cm) 18-gauge wire, silver
- Pair of earring wires
- Roundnose pliers
- Chainnose pliers
- Diagonal wire cutters
- Pencil
- Metal file (optional)

YOU NEED

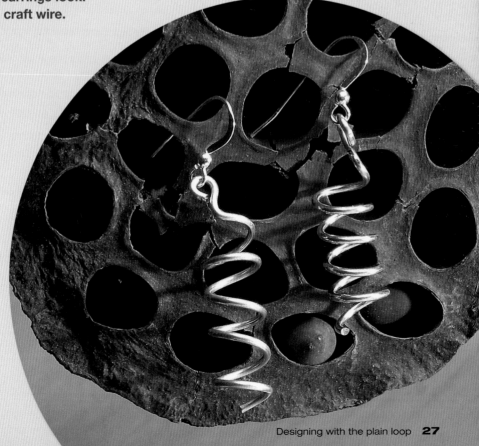

Chapter Two
Designing with the wrapped loop

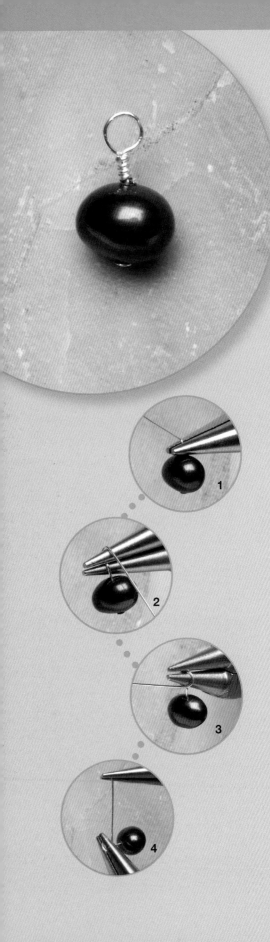

How to make a wrapped loop

1. To make a wrapped loop above a bead, string the bead on a head pin, and trim the wire about 1¼ in. (3.2cm) above the bead. Grasp the wire with chainnose pliers above the bead, placing the wire about ⅛ in. (3mm) from the tips of the pliers. Fold the wire into a right-angle bend over the pliers. (If you're using wire with no bead, grasp the wire 1¼ in. from the end and bend it over the pliers.)

2. Switch to roundnose pliers, and position the jaws in the bend. Bring the end of the wire up and over the top jaw of the pliers, and as far down as you can.

3. Reposition the roundnose pliers so the lower jaw is in the loop. Slide the wire down the jaw so you are working in the same place as in step 2. Curve the wire downward around the bottom of the pliers until the tail is at a right angle to the stem. You've made the first half of a wrapped loop. At this point, you can add dangles to the loop or connect the loop to another element, such as a link of chain.

4. Position your chainnose pliers across the loop as shown. Use a second pair of pliers (roundnose or chainnose) to grasp the end of the wire and wrap it around the stem. Start close to the loop and work toward the bead, keeping your wraps as close together as possible. Fill the gap between the loop and the bead to secure the bead. Trim any excess wire with the diagonal wire cutters, and use chainnose pliers to tuck the end against the stem.

Earring dangle

Wrapped loops are a super-secure way to create a simple earring dangle.

a

1. String a bead on a head pin **(a).**

b

2. Make a wrapped loop above the bead. Repeat to make a second dangle. (Work at the same point on the jaw of your pliers in steps 2 and 3 so both loops will be the same size.) **Open the loop** on an earring wire and add a dangle **(b).** Close the loop. Repeat to make a second earring.

DESIGN IDEA: To me, a wrapped loop looks a lot like the coil you find on some earring wires. When my earring wires are embellished with coils, I often choose a wrapped loop to secure my dangle and repeat the design element.

YOU NEED

• 2 11mm faceted glass round beads
• 2 1½-in. (3.8cm) 22-gauge head pins
• Pair of earring wires
• Roundnose pliers
• Chainnose pliers
• Diagonal wire cutters

When you first start making wrapped loops, you'll feel like you're generating a lot of scrap when you trim the ends of head pins. It's tempting to buy shorter head pins to reduce waste. I lean in the other direction, though, and usually purchase 2- or 3-in. (5 or 7.6cm) head pins. If I'm careful when I'm wrapping, I won't do too much damage to the end, so it can be used for other components, like the plain-loop connectors of the earrings on page 21.

TIP

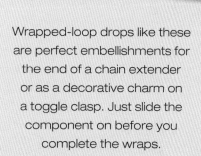

Wrapped-loop drops like these are perfect embellishments for the end of a chain extender or as a decorative charm on a toggle clasp. Just slide the component on before you complete the wraps.

Bead pendant

A wrapped loop can turn a bead into a pendant.

1. String the beads on the decorative head pin **(a).** (You also could use a length of wire with a plain loop at the bottom.)

2. Make a wrapped loop above the top bead and string the pendant on the ribbons **(b). Attach a fold-over crimp** to each ribbon end. Open the jump rings, add a lobster claw clasp to one, and attach a jump ring to each of the crimps. Close the jump rings.

TIP

YOU NEED

- 17mm flat glass bead
- 2 4mm flat spacers
- 2-in. (5cm) decorative head pin
- 2 15-in. (38cm) lengths of ribbon
- 2 fold-over crimps
- 6mm jump ring
- Lobster claw clasp with jump ring
- Roundnose pliers
- Chainnose pliers
- Diagonal wire cutters
- GS-Hypo Cement

You can change the size of your loops by working at different points along the jaws of your roundnose pliers. If your pendant will be strung on a strip of suede, a leather cord, or a ribbon, as in this project, work closer to the handles of the pliers, where the circumference of the jaws is larger. Remember, a bigger loop uses more wire, so allow more than the 1¼ in. (3.2cm) specified in step 1 of "How to make a wrapped loop."

Wrapped

A wrapped loop is an excellent connector because it remains secure, even if there is tension or weight on the connection. I love to connect chain segments with beaded wrapped loops. Begin with a new length of chain, or use this technique to connect leftover pieces of chain.

YOU NEED

- 5 or 6 17 x 15mm saucer-shaped beads
- 10 or 12 4mm spacers
- 18 in. (46cm) 20-gauge half-hard wire, silver
- 18 in. medium, flat, oval curb chain, 3.7 x 7.5mm
- 6mm jump ring (optional)
- Lobster claw clasp with 4mm jump ring
- Roundnose pliers
- Chainnose pliers
- Diagonal wire cutters

DESIGN IDEA: Plain loops are fine for connecting lightweight chain and beads, as in the previous chapter, but for this bolder necklace, I balanced the size of the beads and the weight of the chain with 20-gauge wire and wrapped loops.

loop necklace

1. Cut six 3-in. (7.6cm) wire segments. **Make the first half of a wrapped loop** at one end of each wire segment **(a)**.

2. Cut six 3-in. chain segments. Slide an end link of chain into one loop segment and complete the wraps **(b)**.

3. Add a spacer, a bead, and a spacer, and make the first half of a wrapped loop above the spacer. Pick up an end link of a second piece of chain **(c)** and complete the wraps. Continue until all the chain segments are connected.

4. This necklace should be long enough to slip over your head. To add a clasp, omit the last beaded unit. **Open a 6mm jump ring** and pick up one end of chain. Close the jump ring. Open a 4mm jump ring, add the other end of chain and a lobster claw clasp **(d)**, and close the jump ring.

Here's a smaller-scale version done in gold. I used two additional beaded units close to the clasp. I made one end loop a little larger and used that for the clasp instead of adding another jump ring at the end. For this version, you'll need seven 8mm cathedral-cut crystals, 21 in. (53cm) of gold-filled wire, 15 in. (38cm) of chain cut into five 2½-in. (6.4 cm) lengths, and a lobster claw clasp.

DESIGN IDEA: To make a multistrand necklace, repeat steps 1–3 until you have as many strands as you'd like – all the same length or several graduated lengths. In step 4, pick up all the end links with the 6mm jump ring (use a larger ring if your chain is thicker), and on the other end, pick up all the end links and the clasp.

Multistrand bracelet

This bracelet uses the same techniques as the wrapped-loop necklace. I scaled the design for the wrist and added interest with extra strands.

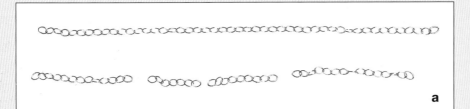

a

1. To determine the length of chain you'll need, measure your wrist, allowing for a loose fit, and measure your clasp. Subtract the clasp length from your wrist measurement and cut four pieces of chain to that length. Cut one of these chain segments into three or four smaller pieces **(a)**.

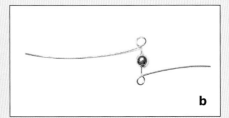

b

2. Make the first half of a wrapped loop on a 3-in. (7.6cm) length of wire. String a bead onto the wire and make the first half of a wrapped loop above the bead **(b)**. Make 12 or more beaded units.

Diagonal wire cutters make nice, sharp cuts and leave an angled tip on the wire. That's good if you need to tuck the end of a wrapped loop, for example. If you need a flush cut (straight across), just turn the cutters 180°. Flush cuts are perfect for the ends of earring wires. Keep in mind that a flush cut to the working wire will leave a diagonal cut on the remaining wire.

This silver version is identical to the gold on the opposite page – the beads are just placed at different intervals. The third version uses gunmetal chain and findings, and 4mm bicone crystals instead of round beads.

- 36 in. (.9m) 24-gauge half-hard wire, gold filled
- 28 in. (71cm) 3mm cable chain, gold filled
- 12 or more 3–6mm round beads, gold filled
- 2 4mm jump rings, gold filled
- Lobster claw clasp with 3mm jump ring, gold filled
- Roundnose pliers
- Chainnose pliers
- Diagonal wire cutters

YOU NEED

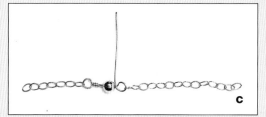
c

d

3. String the end link of a small chain segment to one open loop and complete the wraps. Add a second chain segment to the other end and complete the wraps **(c)**. Continue until all of the small segments are connected with beaded units.

4. Repeat step 3 with the three remaining lengths of chain, cutting each length as you did in step 1. Stagger the lengths of the smaller segments and the placement and size of the beads **(d)**.

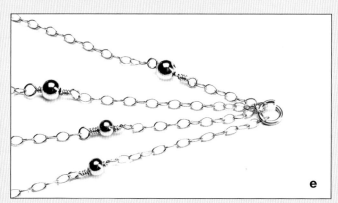
e

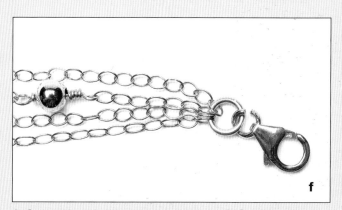
f

5. Double check the lengths of the segments and trim to make even, if necessary. **Open a 4mm jump ring** and connect the four end links of chain **(e)**. Close the jump ring. Repeat on the other side.

6. Open a 3mm jump ring and attach the lobster claw clasp and one end of the bracelet **(f)**. Close the jump ring.

Cluster bracelet

Wrapped loops are strong and secure, so they make excellent connections for charm-style bracelets. This design is a favorite, and I've made it many ways – with crystals, with iridescent glass beads, with pearls, and in all silver. It looks great with beads as small as 4mm and as large as 15mm. I especially like a variety of sizes together. If you'd like an airier feel, try a single bead on a single link, as in the red bracelet on page 37.

- 7 in. (18cm) medium cable chain, 5.6 x 7.6mm
- 100–125 3–6mm round beads, gold filled and silver
- 100–125 1½-in. (3.8cm) head pins
- 2 5mm jump rings
- Toggle clasp, gold filled or silver
- Roundnose pliers
- Chainnose pliers
- Diagonal wire cutters

YOU NEED

Larger loops give more flexibility and swing to your dangles. Just work a little farther down the jaws (closer to the handles) of your roundnose pliers.

TIP

1. To determine the length of chain you'll need, measure your wrist, allowing for a loose fit, and measure the clasp. Subtract the clasp length from your wrist measurement and cut a piece of chain to that length.

a

2. String a bead on a headpin and **make the first half of a wrapped loop** above the bead. Make about 25 beaded units, varying the size of the beads **(a)**. If you'd like, string two or three beads on a headpin – there are no hard-and-fast rules!

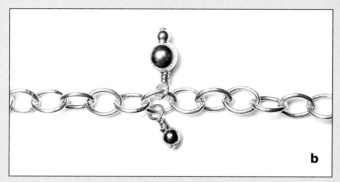

b

3. Beginning at the midpoint of the chain segment, attach a beaded unit to a chain link and complete the wraps. Attach a second bead unit to the other side of the same link, and complete the wraps **(b)**. I like to balance a larger bead on one side of a link with a smaller bead on the other. You may put three or four beaded units on each link – it just depends on how full you'd like your bracelet to be.

4. Continue adding beads, working out from the center in each direction. When you've used up the beaded units you made in step 2, make some more. I find it's less tiring to switch back and forth between making the units and adding them to the chain. You'll ultimately make and attach about 100 beaded units. For maximum fullness, work on both sides of the chain when you attach the dangles.

c

5. When the chain is as full as you'd like, attach the clasp: **Open a jump ring,** and string the end link of chain and a clasp half **(c)**. Close the jump ring. Repeat on the other side with a second jump ring and the remaining clasp half.

Check for rough ends and tuck them in as you finish wrapping. It's much harder to go back and check all of them at the end (despite your good intentions), and you don't want to snag your favorite sweater the first time you wear your beautiful dangles.

TIP

This airy version alternates six 10mm diagonally drilled millefiori cubes with seven 4mm bicone crystals linked to 9 in. (23cm) of chain. A lobster claw clasp is attached to one end, and a 4mm crystal dangle to the other. It's adjustable – just catch the clasp in any link of the chain.

Clusters of lustrous glass beads in several sizes create a colorful version of this bracelet. This variation pairs 4mm, 6mm, and 8mm beads on each dangle. You can see another combination on page 5.

Sunshine anytime sun catcher

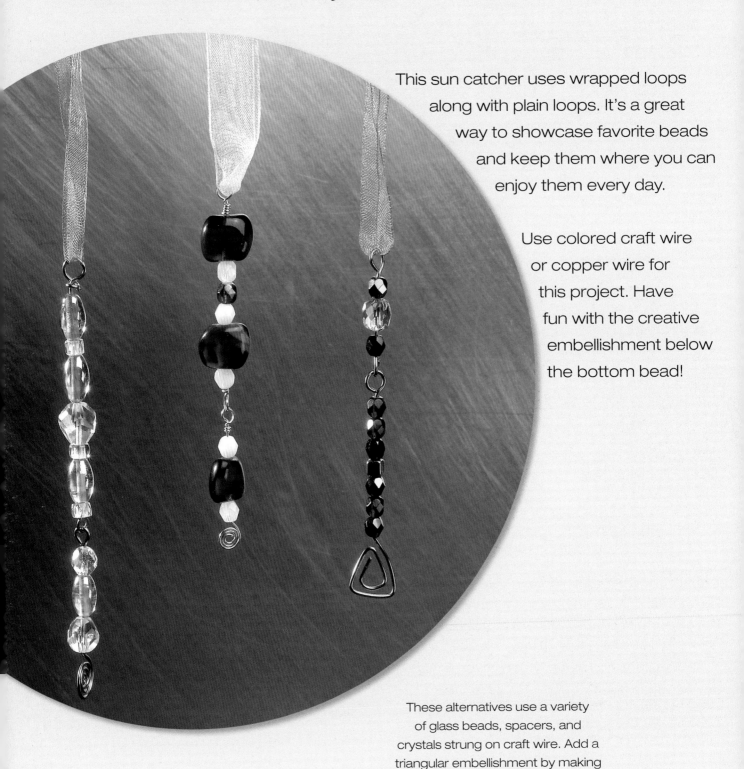

This sun catcher uses wrapped loops along with plain loops. It's a great way to showcase favorite beads and keep them where you can enjoy them every day.

Use colored craft wire or copper wire for this project. Have fun with the creative embellishment below the bottom bead!

These alternatives use a variety of glass beads, spacers, and crystals strung on craft wire. Add a triangular embellishment by making angled bends with chainnose pliers.

- assortment of small and large glass beads
- flat spacer beads
- 14 in. (36cm) craft wire
- 1 ft. (30cm) ribbon
- Chainnose pliers
- Roundnose pliers
- Diagonal wire cutters

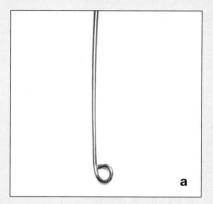

1. Cut a 6-in. (15cm) length of wire. Use your roundnose pliers to make a tiny loop at the end of the wire **(a)**.

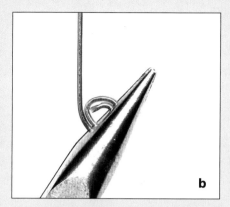

2. Use chainnose pliers and your fingers to gently shape the wire around the loop into a spiral **(b)**.

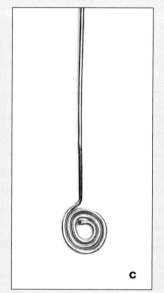

3. When the spiral is complete, use chainnose pliers to make a sharp bend in the wire **(c)**. String a few beads on the wire, and **make a wrapped loop** above the top bead **(d)**.

4. Cut a second piece of wire about 4 in. (10cm) long. **Make a plain loop** at one end. String some beads, and make a plain loop above the beads. Cut a third piece of wire, about 4 in. long. Make a plain loop at one end. String some beads, and make a wrapped loop above the beads. Connect the units **(e)** and finish the wraps.

DESIGN IDEA: Sometimes you'll use plain loops because you want delicate connections that don't show a lot of metal. Sometimes you'll use wrapped loops because you'd like some wire to show or you need a secure connection. Sometimes, as in this project, you'll find the best results come from combining the two.

5. String a ribbon through the top wrapped loop **(f)**. Tie the ribbon ends with an **overhand knot**.

How to wrap a top-drilled bead

Early in my beading days, I fell in love with some darling little teardrops at my local bead store, and I thought they would make perfect earrings. Later I realized the hole in the bead was drilled horizontally through the top. Up to that point, I had used only vertically drilled beads and had no idea how to make my little drops work! Away they went until I learned a little more.

1. Cut a 3-in. (7.6cm) length of wire, and center a top-drilled bead on the wire. Bend each side upward to form a squared-off U shape. Leave a tiny bit of room for the bead to move – about 1mm.

2. Cross the wires into an X above the bead.

3. Use chainnose pliers to bend one wire up and one wire to the side. They'll form a right angle at their intersection.

4. Wrap the horizontal wire around the vertical wire as in a wrapped loop. Make two or three wraps and trim the wrapped wire.

To make a dangle, you can make a plain loop directly above the wraps, or you can make a wrapped loop above the wraps. The tricky part about a wrapped loop is that you want the top wraps to meet the bottom wraps. Not only is this hard to do, but you end up with a bead that looks like it has six or more wraps above it – that's a lot of metal showing!

DESIGN IDEA: If you choose to make a wrapped loop above the wraps, use a slightly thinner wire, such as 24-gauge, for less bulk.

Charming

I wanted the security of wrapped-loop connections in this bracelet so I didn't have to worry about it snagging on anything. I knew my wraps probably wouldn't meet perfectly every time, so I added a crystal between the bottom and the top wraps.

1. To determine the length of chain you'll need, measure your wrist, allowing for a loose fit, and measure the clasp. Subtract the clasp length from your wrist measurement and cut a piece of chain to that length.

2. Count the links and decide how many dangles you want to have. I put a dangle on every other link from the center out. **Wrap above the top-drilled beads** to make the dangle units.

3. String a crystal above the wraps on a bead unit **(a)**.

teardrop bracelet

- 14 8mm Czech glass drops
- 7 3mm bicone crystals, fuchsia AB
- 7 3mm bicone crystals, crystal
- 14 28-gauge head pins, silver
- 7–8 in. (18–20cm) medium cable heavyweight chain, 6.2 x 8.1mm, 20-gauge
- 2 5mm jump rings
- Toggle clasp

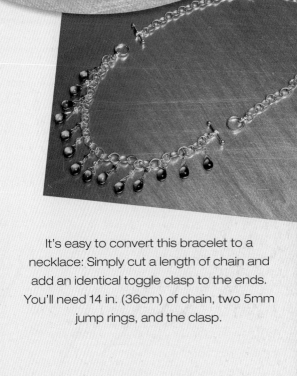

4. Make the first half of a wrapped loop above the crystal. Attach a bead unit to the center link of chain **(b)** and complete the wrapped loop.

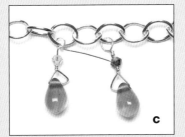

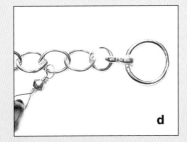

5. Skip a link and add a second dangle (I changed crystal color for interest) **(c)**. Repeat until you've attached all the dangles.

6. Attach the clasp: **Open a jump ring** and string the end link of chain and a clasp half **(d)**. Close the jump ring. Repeat on the other side with a second jump ring and the remaining clasp half.

It's easy to convert this bracelet to a necklace: Simply cut a length of chain and add an identical toggle clasp to the ends. You'll need 14 in. (36cm) of chain, two 5mm jump rings, and the clasp.

Briolette

Briolettes are faceted, teardrop-shaped gemstone beads. Because of their shape, they are most appealing to me when used as dangles.

YOU NEED

necklace

- 12 x 12mm briolette
- Strand 4mm potato pearls
- 10 6mm round pearls
- 2 crimp beads
- 4 2mm round beads
- 3-link segment of medium cable heavyweight chain, 6.2 x 8.1mm, 20-gauge
- 1 26-gauge 2-in. (5cm) head pin
- Flexible beading wire, .014 or .015
- Roundnose pliers
- Chainnose pliers
- Crimping pliers
- Diagonal wire cutters

NECKLACE

a

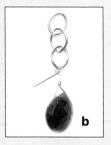

b

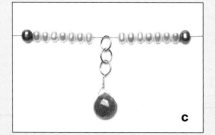

c

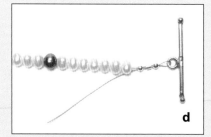

d

1. Make a set of wraps above the briolette. Make the first half of a wrapped loop above the wraps, perpendicular to the triangle above the bead **(a).**

2. Link the loop to the end of a three-link chain segment **(b)** and complete the wraps.

3. Determine the finished length of your necklace, add 6 in. (15cm), and cut a piece of flexible beading wire to that length. Center the chain segment on the wire. String seven 4mm beads and one 6mm bead on each side of the chain **(c).**

4. Repeat until the necklace is the desired length, ending with seven 4mm beads. On each end, string a 2mm round, a crimp bead, a 2mm round, and half the clasp. Go back through the beads just strung **(d).** Check the fit and add or remove beads, if necessary. Tighten the wires and **make folded crimps** in the crimp beads. Trim the excess wire.

dangle necklace and earrings

EARRINGS

a

1. Make a set of wraps above a briolette and string a 3mm bicone crystal **(a).**

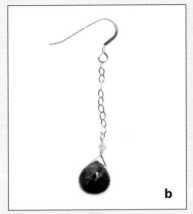

b

2. Make a plain loop above the crystal and connect the loop to one end of a chain segment. Connect the other end of the chain to an earring wire **(b).** Make a second earring to match the first.

earrings

- 2 12 x 12mm briolettes
- 2 3mm crystals
- 2 26-gauge head pins
- 2 10-link segments of small, flat cable chain, 2 x 3.4mm, 30-gauge
- Pair of earring wires
- Roundnose pliers
- Chainnose pliers
- Diagonal wire cutters

YOU NEED

These variations have five 8 x 6mm briolettes in the dangles and accent beads on either side of the chain.

Chapter Three
Designing with jump rings

Rosette bracelet

Make rosettes by linking three jump rings, and then string them all into this charming bracelet.

- 10 10mm 16-gauge jump rings, gold filled
- 27 7mm 16-gauge jump rings, silver
- 2 5mm jump rings, gold filled
- Toggle clasp
- 2 pairs of chainnose pliers

YOU NEED

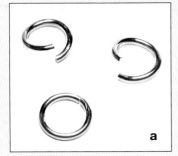

1. Close one 7mm jump ring and open two **(a)**.

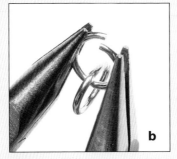

2. Pick up the closed ring with an open ring, and close the second ring **(b)**.

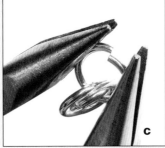

3. Pick up both closed rings with the third open ring, and close the third **(c)**. Repeat to make a total of nine rosettes **(d)**.

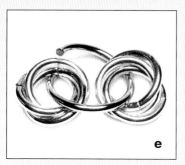

e

4. Open a 10mm jump ring and pick up two rosettes **(e)**. Close the jump ring.

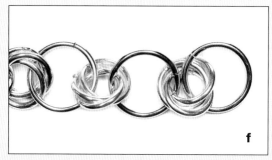

f

5. Open a 10mm jump ring, pick up one strung rosette and a new one, and close the jump ring. Repeat to string all the rosettes, and end with a 10mm jump ring on each end **(f)**. Check the fit to see if your bracelet is the desired length, less the length of the clasp, and add or remove any links, if necessary.

g

6. Open a 5mm jump ring and connect an end link with a clasp half **(g)**. Repeat on the other end.

Most of the bracelets in this chapter also can be necklaces. You'll need a little more than double the materials to extend the designs by about 8 in. (20cm).

TIP

How to open and close a jump ring

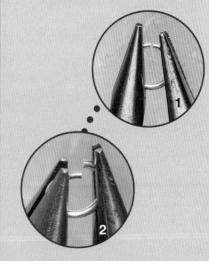

1. Hold the jump ring with two pairs of pliers, as shown.

2. To open the ring, bring one pair of pliers toward you and push the other pair away.

You can string materials on the open ring, if desired. To close, reverse the steps above.

Rose-and-gold bracelet

Jump rings are utilitarian connectors, as demonstrated in this pretty bracelet.

YOU NEED

- 10 5mm crystals, lentil shaped
- 30 in. (76cm) 22-gauge wire, gold-filled
- 11 4mm jump rings
- Lobster claw clasp
- Roundnose pliers
- Chainnose pliers
- Diagonal wire cutters

a

b

c

1. Cut 10 3-in. (7.6cm) segments of 22-gauge wire. On each segment, **make a wrapped loop** at one end, string a crystal, and make a wrapped loop at the other end **(a)**.

2. Open a jump ring, and connect two bead units **(b)**. Close the jump ring. Repeat until all the bead units are connected.

3. Open a jump ring, and string the end unit and a clasp **(c)**. Close the jump ring. Attach a jump ring to the other end.

YOU NEED

- 6 4mm round beads, garnet
- 12 4 x 2mm spacers, silver
- 12 5mm flat spacers, silver
- 5 charms, Hill Tribes silver
- 7 5mm jump rings, silver
- 36 in. (.9m) 22-gauge wire, silver
- Lobster claw clasp
- Roundnose pliers
- Chainnose pliers
- Diagonal wire cutters

Hang loose bracelet

Jump rings add motion and flexibility to links that could be stiff. I wanted to include charms with my wrapped-loop connections, and linking it all together with jump rings created the swing I was looking for.

a

1. Cut a 3-in. (7.6cm) length of wire. **Make a wrapped loop** at one end, and string a spacer, a 4mm bead, and a spacer. Make a wrapped loop at the other end. Repeat to make six "A" units. Cut a 3-in. length of wire. Make a wrapped loop at one end. String two spacers, and make the first half of a wrapped loop at the other end **(a)**. Repeat to make six "B" units.

b

2. Link the open loop of a "B" to a closed loop of an "A" and complete the wraps **(b)**.

c

3. Open a jump ring. String the end loop of "A", a charm, and a closed loop of another "B" unit **(c)**. Close the jump ring. Repeat steps 2 and 3 until the bracelet is the desired length. Complete the last wraps, if needed.

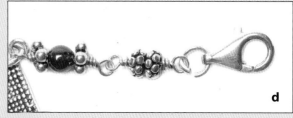

d

4. Open a jump ring, and string the end loop and a clasp **(d)**. Close the jump ring. String a jump ring on the other end.

3 'n' 3 link bracelet

I especially like jump rings in a heavy gauge and on a big scale. This easy project offers different looks by varying the size of rings and type of metals used.

- 24 13mm jump rings, 14-gauge
- 29 8.5mm jump rings, 14-gauge
- Clasp
- 2 pairs of chainnose pliers

YOU NEED

a

1. Close three 8.5mm jump rings and open three 13mm jump rings **(a)**.

b

2. Pick up three closed jump rings with one open jump ring **(b)**. Close the ring. Attach two more jump rings through the three closed rings. You now have two linked sets of three.

This variation combines sets of three 7mm silver jump rings with sets of three 5mm gold rings. Finish with a single 7mm ring on each end and a toggle clasp.

This pattern pairs sets of three 8.5mm jump rings with sets of two 5mm rings. Finish with a single 5mm ring on each end and a lobster claw clasp.

c

This version pairs sets of three 7mm silver jump rings with sets of two 5mm gold-filled jump rings. End with a single 5mm ring on each end.

d

e

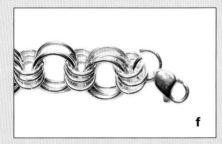

f

3. Pick up the three linked 8.5mm jump rings with a 13mm jump ring **(c)**, and then string three more closed 8.5mm rings **(d)**. Close the jump ring, then add two more 13mm rings. Separate the smaller rings so you have four connected sets of three rings each.

4. Continue until the bracelet is equal to your desired length minus the clasp measurement. End with 8.5mm sets on each end **(e)**.

5. Attach a single 8.5mm jump ring to one end of the bracelet. Repeat on the other side with another 8.5mm jump ring and the clasp **(f)**.

Jump ring necklace

Although this necklace uses three different sizes of jump rings and two different finishes, everything comes together in a clean, timeless style.

YOU NEED

- 13–15 13mm jump rings
- 14–16 8.5mm jump rings
- 20 5mm jump rings
- 7 6mm beads
- 7 1-in. (2.5cm) head pins
- Toggle clasp
- Roundnose pliers
- 2 pairs of chainnose pliers
- Diagonal wire cutters

a

b

c

1. Close 14–16 8.5mm jump rings. Close 13–15 13mm jump rings. Open a 5mm jump ring and link one 8.5mm and one 13mm **(a)**. Close the 5mm. Continue linking rings, alternating small and large, until the necklace is about 1 in. (2.5cm) shorter than the desired length.

2. String a 6mm bead onto a head pin and **make a plain loop** above the bead **(b)**. Make seven units.

3. Open the loop of a bead unit, and attach it to the center 13mm ring **(c)**. Close the loop. Attach the remaining bead units to the 13mm rings on either side of the center.

d

4. Attach one half of the clasp to one end jump ring with a 5mm ring **(d)**. Repeat on the other side.

 TIP

A chain is only as strong as its weakest link. Be sure to close every ring as perfectly as you can. Work slowly and strive for a gapless connection. It's much easier to check each ring as you work than to go back over a piece once it's finished.

Big ring bracelet

Soldered jump rings can save time. In this bracelet, the big links were soldered, so I worked only with the smaller links.

YOU NEED

- 7 22mm round links, gold filled
- 14 7mm 16-gauge jump rings, silver
- 15mm lobster claw clasp
- 2 pairs of chainnose pliers

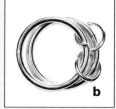

1. Open a 7mm jump ring, and string two 22mm rings **(a)**. Close the 7mm ring. Repeat to add a second 7mm ring **(b)**.

2. Separate the large rings. Open a 7mm ring, and string one end of the unit from step 1 and a new 22mm ring **(c)**. Close the jump ring. Repeat with a second 7mm ring. Continue until the bracelet is your desired length (minus the clasp measurement).

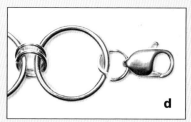

3. Open a 7mm ring. String the end 22mm ring and a lobster claw clasp **(d)**. Close the ring. Add a 7mm ring to the other end.

TIP

Soldered, open, or spring? When you're choosing a ring to use opposite a lobster claw clasp, select a soldered jump ring or a split ring for a strung project, such as one on flexible beading wire. Why? Because no matter how well you close an open jump ring, the beading wire can slip through the tiny space and the necklace or bracelet will fall off. With a design that uses chain, any of the styles will work.

Chapter Four
Designing with chain

Chain styles

I love chain. It provides tremendous versatility and gives a polished and professional look to finished jewelry. Chain can get you places that simple stringing can't – it provides options for drape and dangle and even density. Did I mention that I love chain?

Chain comes in a wide variety of styles, named for the shapes of the links. You'll also find descriptive words for the size of the link, the weight of the wire, and any finish on the link. For example, "medium textured 3 x 5mm curb" means that the wire is of medium weight (about 22-gauge), the link is a slightly twisted oval about 3mm wide by 5mm long, and the wire has been textured or brushed.

You'll also have a choice of metals, ranging from precious metals, like sterling silver and gold filled, to base metal and other less-expensive options.

In the photo below, you'll see a variety of my favorite chain styles. From top to bottom: cable, three styles of long-and-short, cable, rolo, drawn cable, figure-eight, cable, curb, and textured curb.

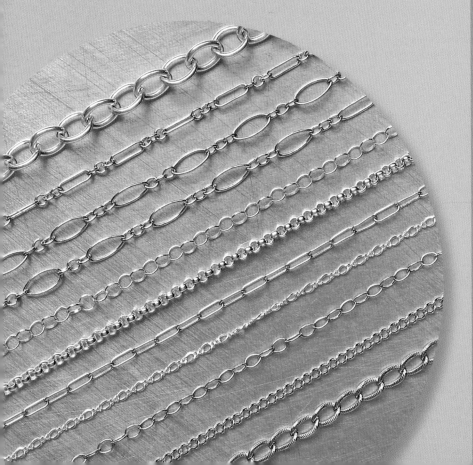

Chain reaction bracelet

At first glance, it may not be obvious how I created this bracelet. I wanted a simple but hefty bracelet to showcase large beads, but it had to be comfortable and easy to wear. Large-link chain collapsed over elastic gave me just what I was looking for.

1. Measure your wrist, add 5 in. (13cm), and double the measurement. Cut a piece of elastic to that length. Center a twisted wire beading needle on the elastic and tape the ends together.

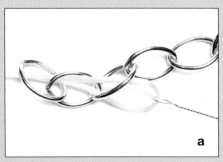

a

2. Cut four 5-in. segments of chain. String one chain segment by threading the elastic through each link **(a)**. Slide the chain down the elastic as you work.

b

3. String beads as desired (b).

c

4. Continue stringing chain, alternating chain segments and beads. Remove the tape. Tie the ends together with a **surgeon's knot (c)**.

d

5. Glue the knot (d), trim the ends, and slide the knot into the chain to hide it.

See a variation in silver on page 5.

TIP

Save your extra chain! One link is a substitute for a soldered jump ring. Three links can suspend a pendant (see page 42). Five links make a necklace or toggle extender. More than that, and you're on your way to a mixed-metal mélange!

Pearl scrunchie bracelet

Silver and pearls are usually elegant, but this treatment introduces some welcome funkiness. The elastic thread makes the chain hug the pearls, almost like a frame. I love the waviness created by the tension.

- 10 8mm (large) pearls
- 27 4mm (small) pearls
- 8 in. (20cm) 3mm cable chain
- 2 5mm jump rings
- Toggle clasp
- Ribbon elastic
- Twisted wire beading needle
- G-S Hypo Cement
- Scissors

a

1. Cut a 25-in. (64cm) length of ribbon elastic. Center it on a twisted-wire beading needle, and tape the ends together. Thread one link of chain and one 8mm pearl **(a)**.

b

2. Skip three links of chain and come through the next link. Pull the elastic tight, leaving a 5-in. (13cm) tail. Thread a 4mm pearl **(b)**.

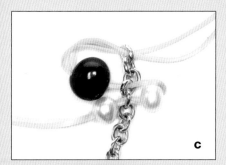

c

d

e

3. Come through the next link of chain. Add a 4mm pearl **(c)**. Come through the next link of chain. Repeat with a third 4mm pearl and a third link of chain.

4. String one 8mm pearl and repeat steps 2 and 3. Continue this sequence until you reach the end of the chain.

5. Tie the elastic tail around the last link of chain with a **surgeon's knot (d)**. Glue the knot and trim the end. Repeat on the other end.

6. Open a 5mm jump ring, and string an end link of chain and half the clasp **(e)**. Close the jump ring. Repeat on the other end.

DESIGN IDEA: Design is subjective. Sometimes you'll just know when something is – or isn't – working. Artists speak of being inspired by the beads. Often I sit down to work with a clear plan in mind, and the resulting jewelry couldn't be further from my intention. That makes me believe in muses, and reminds me that even a book about design can't explain everything!

This version uses 5mm cable chain and alternating colors of 8mm pearls. Because the scale is larger, it can slide on without a clasp – just tie the elastic ends together to complete the circle.

Chain-over-leather necklace

When I started working with leather, I had a hard time finding accent beads with holes large enough to string over the cord. Chain came to my rescue – by weaving it over the leather, I created the accent I wanted. Dropping a link along the way created a built-in bail, and a favorite design was born.

CAL (in supply list, above) is short for Comet Argent Light, a bright silver coating that is applied over half the bead for a two-tone effect.

TIP

a

1. Determine the finished length of your necklace, subtract 1 in. (2.5cm) for the clasp, and cut a piece of leather to that length. Cut a 35-link length of chain. String the chain on the leather as shown for five links, then skip a link. Repeat four times, and string the final five links of chain **(a)**.

This variation uses 8mm focal beads accented with 4mm jet and garnet bicone crystals over white leather.

b

2a. String a decorative head pin with a 4mm bicone, a 10mm bead, and a 4mm bicone. **Make the first half of a wrapped loop** above the top bead. Repeat to make three dangles.

2b. String a decorative head pin with a 4mm bicone, a 6mm bicone, and a 4mm bicone. Make the first half of a wrapped loop above the top bead. Make two dangles **(b)**.

c

3. Attach a dangle from step 2a to the center dropped link **(c)**. Complete the wraps.

d

4. Attach a dangle from step 2b next to the center dangle **(d)**. Complete the wraps.

5. Attach the remaining dangles to the remaining dropped links.

e

6. Apply GS-Hypo cement to one end of the leather cord, and insert the cord into a fold-over crimp end. With chainnose pliers, **fold the crimp** over the cord **(e)**. Repeat on the other end.

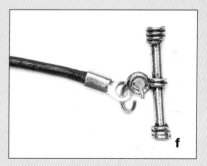

f

7. Open a jump ring, and string the loop of one crimp end and a clasp half **(f)**. Close the jump ring.

8. On the other side, open a jump ring, string the remaining clasp half and the other crimp end loop, and close the jump ring.

Chain V necklace

It's so easy to create a pendant with chain – and easy to modify. Go longer or shorter, or try using more or fewer lengths of chain. Just keep the same proportion between the strands for a smooth, graduated V.

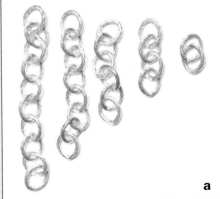

a

1. Determine the finished length of your necklace. Subtract the clasp measurement, and cut a piece of chain to that length.

2. Cut one 10-link segment, two 8-link segments, two 6-link segments, two 4-link segments, and two 2-link segments **(a)**.

YOU NEED

- 2 or more ft. (61cm+) medium textured cable chain, heavyweight, 3.8 x 4.7mm, 21-gauge
- 13mm 14-gauge jump ring
- 8.5mm 14-gauge jump ring
- 2 4mm jump rings
- 13mm lobster claw clasp
- 2 pairs of chainnose pliers
- Diagonal wire cutters

b

c

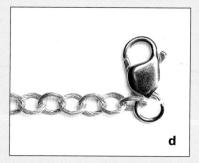

d

DESIGN IDEA: Odds are a good bet when it comes to designing jewelry. Three or five dangles are perfect. Three strands look nicer than two. Odd numbers are fashionable, too – just count the buttons on your favorite coat or cardigan.

3. Open the 13mm jump ring. String 2-link, 4-link, 6-link, 8-link, 10-link, 8-link, 6-link, 4-link, and 2-link segments **(b)**. Close the jump ring.

4. Open the 8.5mm jump ring, and string the pendant and the center link of the necklace chain segment **(c)**. Close the jump ring.

5. Open a 4mm jump ring, attach it to one end of the necklace, and close the jump ring. Open a 4mm jump ring, and attach the link at the other end and a lobster claw clasp **(d)**. Close the jump ring.

These earrings use 3mm cable chain in a pattern of three links, five links, seven links, five links, and three links on a 5mm jump ring. They are linked to the earring wire with a 3mm jump ring. If you skip the 3mm jump ring, the earring design will be visible from the front; with the extra jump ring, it's visible from the side.

Chain lariat

The combination of fine chain, large crystal cubes, and dramatic length makes this a very elegant necklace.

YOU NEED

- 8 or 10mm cube crystal
- 8 or 10mm bicone crystal
- 8 4mm bicone crystals
- 4 3mm bicone crystals
- 14 3mm flat spacers
- 27 in. (69cm) twisted figure-eight chain
- Jump ring
- Loop half of a toggle clasp
- 6 in. (23cm) 24-gauge wire
- 5 2-in. (5cm), 24-gauge head pins
- Roundnose pliers
- Chainnose pliers
- Diagonal wire cutters

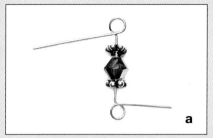

a

1. Cut the chain into three 6-in. (15cm) segments and one 9-in. (23cm) segment. Cut a 2-in. (5cm) length of wire. **Make the first half of a wrapped loop** at one end. String a 4mm spacer, a 4mm bicone, and a 4mm spacer. Make the first half of a wrapped loop at the other end **(a)**. Repeat to make a total of three beaded units.

b

2. Connect two 6-in. chain segments with a unit from step 1 **(b)**. Complete the wraps. Connect a third 6-in. segment with a second unit and complete the wraps. Connect the 9-in. segment with the third bead unit and complete the wraps.

c

3. Attach the loop end of a toggle clasp to the end of the 6-in. chain segment with a jump ring **(c)**.

d

Make the end dangles **(d, clockwise from left):**
4a. On a head pin, string a spacer, a cube, a spacer, an 8mm bicone, a spacer, a 4mm bicone, and a spacer. Make the first half of a wrapped loop above the beads.
4b. On a head pin, string a spacer, a 4mm bicone and a spacer. Make the first half of a wrapped loop above the beads. Repeat to make a second unit.
4c. On a head pin, string a 3mm bicone, a 4mm bicone, and a 3mm bicone. Make the first half of a wrapped loop above the beads. Repeat to make a second unit.

e

f

g

h

5. Pass the long chain end through the toggle loop **(e)**.
6. Attach the dangle from step 4a to the end of the chain **(f)**.
7. Attach the dangle from step 4b to the first small link. Attach the dangle from 4c to the third small link **(g)**.
8. Skip the twisted link, and repeat step 7 to attach the two remaining dangles **(h)**.

It's easy to give your lariat an antique look. Just seal it in an airtight container with the yolk of a hardboiled egg for about 24 hours. The sulfur in the yolk will oxidize the silver, gradually turning the surface black. Gently buff with a polishing cloth to bring out the highlights.

TIP

Dressy drop

This faux lariat works at any length. It looks pretty with a formal neckline, but it also works with an open-collar blouse.

1. String a 6mm bicone, 8mm round, and 3mm bicone on a head pin. **Make a plain loop** above the beads **(a, left)**. Repeat to make a second beaded unit. String a 3mm bicone, a 4mm bicone, and a 3mm bicone on a 3-in. (7.6cm) length of wire. **Make the first half of a wrapped loop** on each end **(a, right)**. Repeat to make four units.

YOU NEED

• 2 8mm round crystals
• 2 6mm bicone crystals
• 4 4mm bicone crystals
• 10 3mm bicone crystals
• 2-hole spacer
• 20 in. (51cm) small lightweight cable chain, 1.5 x 2mm
• 1 ft. 22-gauge wire or 4 3-in. (7.6cm) head pins
• 2 1 ½-in. (3.8cm) head pins
• 2 5mm jump rings
• Clasp
• Roundnose pliers
• Chainnose pliers
• Diagonal wire cutters

DESIGN IDEA: The wrapped-loop detail on both sides of the clasp adds sparkle at the back – a nice touch if you're wearing an up-do!

2. Cut a 1-in. (2.5cm) length of chain, a 1½-in. (3.8cm) length of chain, and two 8½-in. (21.6cm) lengths of chain. Attach one plain-loop unit from step 1 to the end of the 1-in. chain **(b)**.

3. Attach a wrapped-loop unit from step 1 to the other end. Complete the wraps. Attach one end of the 8½-in. length of chain to the open loop **(c)**, and complete the wraps.

4. Repeat step 2 with the 1½-in. length of chain and the remaining plain-loop unit from step 1. Repeat step 3 with a wrapped-loop unit and the remaining 8½-in. length of chain.

5. Pass the ends of one of the 8½-in. chains through the spacer **(d)**. Repeat with the remaining 8½-in. chain.

6. Attach a wrapped-loop unit to each end and complete all the wraps. **Open a jump ring**, and string the clasp and an end loop **(e)**. Close the jump ring. Attach a jump ring to the other end loop.

Chain drape

The cascading centerpiece of this necklace deserves to be front and center, so keep the beaded portion at choker length. I love the fluid lines of this tiny-link chain, but a larger link could be equally effective.

YOU NEED

- 5 18mm donuts
- 76 5mm round beads
- 4 6mm round beads
- 4 3mm beads
- 2 crimp beads
- Clasp
- 20–30 in. (51–76cm) fine, lightweight rolo chain, 1.5mm
- Flexible beading wire, .014 or .015
- Chainnose pliers or crimping pliers
- Diagonal wire cutters

1. Determine the finished length of the beaded portion of your necklace, add 6 in. (15cm), and cut a piece of flexible beading wire to that length. String the end link of chain onto the flexible beading wire **(a)**.

2. String a donut onto the chain, and drape the chain about 1 in. (2.5cm) below the wire. Bring the chain back up, and string a link onto the beading wire **(b)**.

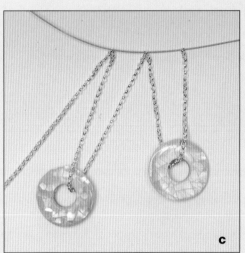

3. Repeat with the remaining donuts. Stagger the lengths of the drapes and place the longest drape in the center **(c, d)**. Trim any excess chain.

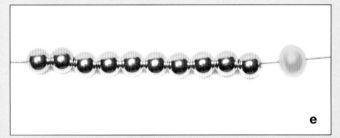

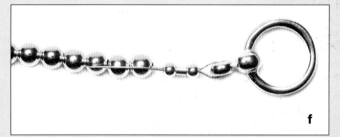

4. On each side of the centerpiece, string 10 5mm beads and a 6mm bead **(e)**. Repeat once.

5. Continue stringing 5mm beads on each side until the necklace is within 1 in. of your desired length. On each end, string a 3mm bead, a crimp bead, a 3mm bead, and half the clasp. Go back through the beads just strung **(f)**. Tighten the wires and check the fit. Add or remove beads, if necessary. **Crimp the crimp beads**, and trim the excess wire.

Briolette necklace and earrings

Faceted briolettes add an air of elegance to this set, and chain gives a tassel-like effect to the center.

Necklace
- 12mm round bead
- 3 8 x 6mm briolettes
- 5 3mm crystals
- 2 3mm flat spacers
- 20 in. (51cm) small, flat, lightweight cable chain
- 14 in. (15cm) wire, 24-gauge, silver
- 2 in. (5cm) 22-gauge wire, silver
- 2 4mm jump rings
- Lobster claw clasp
- Chainnose pliers
- Roundnose pliers
- Diagonal wire cutters

NECKLACE

a

1. Cut a 17-in. (43cm) length of chain, and cut three additional lengths: 1½ in. (3.8cm), 1 in. (2.5cm), and ½ in. (1.3cm)

2. Cut a 4-in. (10cm) piece of wire. **String a briolette, and make a set of wraps above it**. String a 3mm crystal, and **make the first half of a wrapped loop** above the crystal **(a)**. Repeat to make three units.

b

c

d

This necklace variation uses a 15-in. (38cm) length of chain, a 9mm bead in the center, and no small spacers. The faceted briolettes are labradorite.

3. Attach one briolette unit to the end of each of the smaller lengths of chain, and **complete the wraps (b)**.

4. Cut a 2-in. (5cm) length of wire (or trim the end from a head pin). Make the first half of a wrapped loop at one end, and string the three beaded chain segments from step 3 **(c)**. Complete the wraps.

5. String a 3mm crystal, a 3mm flat spacer, a 12mm bead, a 3mm flat spacer, and a 3mm crystal **(d)**.

e

f

6. Make a plain loop above the beaded unit from step 5, and attach it to the center link of the 17-in. (43cm) chain segment **(e)**. Close the loop.

7. Open a 4mm jump ring, and string the clasp and an end link of chain **(f)**. Close the jump ring. Open a 4mm jump ring, and attach it to the other end of the chain.

EARRINGS

a

1. Cut a 5-link segment of chain **(a)**.

b

2. Cut a 2-in. (5cm) length of wire. Make a set of wraps above a briolette, and make the first half of a wrapped loop above the wraps. Repeat to make three dangles **(b)**.

YOU NEED

Earrings
- 6 8 x 6mm briolettes
- 1 ft. (30cm) 24-gauge wire, silver
- 2 five-link segments of small, flat, lightweight cable chain, 2 x 3.4mm
- Pair of earring wires
- Chainnose pliers
- Roundnose pliers
- Diagonal wire cutters

c

3. Attach a dangle to the end link of chain, and complete the wraps **(c)**.

d

4. Skip a link, and attach a dangle to the next link of chain **(d)**. Complete the wraps.

e

5. Skip a link, and attach a dangle to the next link of chain (on the opposite side of the link from step 4) **(e)**. Complete the wraps.

f

6. Open the loop of an earring wire, and connect the end link of chain **(f)**. Close the loop. Repeat to make a second earring.

Purse-onality

I don't mind buying my purses and totes off the rack, but a plain bag always begs for a personal touch. This purse charm adds the personality I crave, and because it's removable, I can change it from season to season.

- 5–7 6–10mm beads or charms
- 6mm round bead
- 5 x 10mm cone
- 5–7 4mm jump rings
- 5–7 1½-in. (3.8cm) head pins
- 6 in. (15cm) 20-gauge wire
- 25–30 in. (64–76cm) chain
- 25mm lobster claw clasp
- Roundnose pliers
- Chainnose pliers
- Diagonal wire cutters

YOU NEED

DESIGN IDEA: I'm all for putting the flash outside my purse and keeping more cash inside. Antique copper or gunmetal finish components look great in these charms, and they're economical, too.

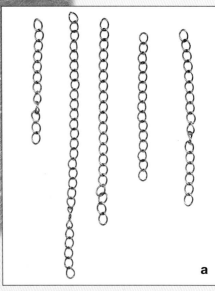
a

1. Cut 5–7 lengths of chain, between 3 and 6 in. (7.6 to 15cm) long **(a)**.

b

c

2. Open a jump ring and attach a charm, or string beads on head pins and **make the first half of a wrapped loop** above the beads. Attach the jump ring or the loop to an end link of chain **(b, c)**. Close the loop or ring.

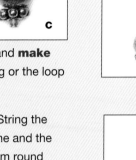

3. Slide the tube bead onto a chain after you've attached a wrapped-loop dangle **(d)**.

d

4. Make the first half of a wrapped loop on the 6-in. wire. String the end links of chain on the loop **(e)**, and complete the wraps.

e

5. String the cone and the 6mm round bead **(f)**.

f

6. Make the first half of a wrapped loop above the bead, and string the clasp **(g)**. Complete the wraps.

g

Dramatic dangle earrings

Delicate chain makes these earrings dramatic without being over the top. This is a great way to use leftovers from earlier projects. Attach crystals and spacers to varied lengths of chain with plain loops. Pull it all together with a beaded double loop at the top.

Chapter Five
Designing with spacers

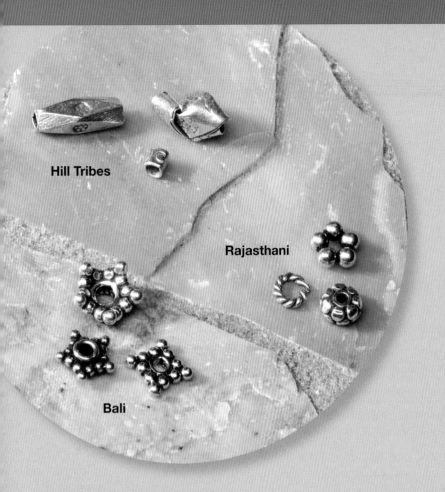

Hill Tribes

Rajasthani

Bali

Big bead necklace

Bold color packs a punch, and I love how this necklace stands out from a monochromatic outfit. But too much color would have been, well, too much. So I chose to add a lot of silver accents, and spacers gave me flexibility in controlling length and balance that I wouldn't have had with oblong beads.

Spacer beads

A spacer is any bead that separates the primary beads in a design. Although you'll find other types of spacers, for the projects in this book, choose finishes such as silver, gold, vermeil, and copper. You'll see shapes such as round, square, flat, stacked, oval, and star, in sizes ranging from tiny 2mm to commanding 8mm or larger. Bead caps are curved spacers that are used in pairs to cradle a bead.

Certain regions are known for certain types of silver beads, and you'll often see these when you go to buy spacers. Some of the most common are:

Hill Tribes silver: These beads are handmade by the Karen Hill Tribes in the mountains of northern Thailand. The silver content of these beads is typically 95–99% (higher than the 92.5% content of sterling silver), so these beads are whiter and slightly softer than sterling.

Bali silver: You'll recognize these beads by their raised decoration, often in the form of tiny balls of silver, and the oxidized or blackened finish that emphasizes the detail. They are handmade from sterling silver.

Rajasthani silver is handmade in India and has a lustrous finish.

Here's another way to handle a lot of color without going overboard: Spread out these pretty 12mm crackle beads with lots of 4mm spacers, a few 6mm bicones, and some 4mm gemstones for accents. You'll need 8 large beads, 9 bicone crystals, 18 gemstones, 180 4mm flat spacers, and the same finishing material as the necklace above.

1. Determine the finished length of your necklace, add 6 in. (15cm), and cut a piece of flexible beading wire to that length.

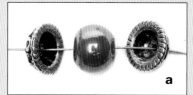

2. Center a bead cap, a glass bead, and a bead cap on the wire **(a)**.

3. On each side, string a pearl, three spacers, and a pearl **(b)**. Repeat steps 2 and 3 three times, then repeat step 2 so your pattern ends with a capped bead on each end.

4. On each end, string three spacers and a pearl **(c)**. Repeat until your necklace is about 1 in. shorter than the desired length.

5. On each end, string a 2mm bead, a crimp bead, a 2mm bead, and half the clasp. Go back through the beads just strung **(d)**, and tighten the wire.

6. Check the fit, and add or remove beads, if necessary. **Crimp the crimp bead**, and trim the excess wire.

Earrings with big beads need a visual anchor. Use a 6mm bicone above the bead and layer 4mm spacers between everything. Finish with a wrapped loop and a pair of earring wires.

DESIGN IDEA: Flat or folded crimps? It's a matter of taste. A flattened crimp tube makes a neat square and it looks nice bracketed with two round beads. Folded crimps can be hidden in beads with large holes. Sometimes I bracket a folded crimp with two tiny flat spacers instead of beads for a barbell look. See pages 92–93 for details on making both kinds of crimps.

Mother's bracelet

Tiny letters and birthstone crystals keep my daughters close to me even though they are practically off on their own. I wanted to make the scale of this bracelet small. I stacked different sizes of spacers to get the look I desired – easier than searching for a bead that's the perfect size. Using spacers also gave me flexibility in finishing the strands evenly, since each name has a different number of letter beads.

TIP

When crimping multistrand necklaces or bracelets, crimp each end of one strand at a time (instead of crimping all on one side first) for a better fit.

1. Determine the finished length of your bracelet. Add 5 in. (13cm) and cut a piece of beading wire to this length. Repeat for each strand, cutting one strand for each name you plan to string.

a

2. String an alternating pattern of round spacers and letter beads on each strand. Center the beads on the wires **(a)**.

b

For this project, I chose crystals in colors that matched my daughters' birthstones. Follow my stringing patterns or feel free to improvise!

TIP

3. On each side of the letter beads, string a pattern of spacers and crystals **(b)**.

c

4. Repeat the pattern until each strand is about 1 in. (2.5cm) shorter than the desired length. On each end of each strand, string a round spacer, a crimp, a round spacer, and half the clasp **(c)**. Go back through the beads just strung, tighten the wires, check the fit, and add or remove any beads, if necessary. **Crimp the crimp beads**, and trim the excess wire.

Hill Tribes silver necklaces

You've heard the expression, "the whole is greater than the sum of the parts"? These designs, made up almost entirely of spacer beads, are a good example. Combining the spacers adds interest, the long spacers provide length, and a few accent beads complete the design. Because these necklaces use similar beads, they can be worn together; use a smaller clasp and vary the lengths.

1. Determine the finished length of your necklace, add 6 in. (15cm), and cut a piece of beading wire to that length. My necklaces range from 15–17 in. (38-43cm).

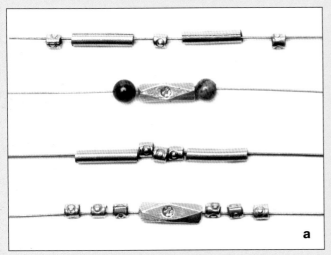

2. String a pattern of spacers **(a)** until the necklace is about 1 in. (2.5cm) shorter than your desired length.

3. On each end, string a 2mm round spacer, a crimp bead, a 2mm spacer, and a jump ring or half the clasp. Go back through the beads just strung **(b)**, check the fit, and add or remove beads, if necessary. Tighten the wires, **crimp the crimp beads**, and trim the excess wire.

4. To make an optional extender, string a 3mm round, a 4mm round, and a 3mm round on a head pin. **Make the first half of a wrapped loop** above the beads. Attach to a 2 in. (5cm) length of chain, and complete the wraps. Substitute the chain for the jump ring in step 3.

YOU NEED

Silver necklace
- 8 10mm rectangle spacers
- 14 10mm tube spacers
- 69 2mm tube spacers
- 4 2mm round spacer beads
- 2 crimp beads
- 5mm jump ring
- Clasp

Silver and blue necklace
- 8 10mm rectangle spacers
- 18 10 mm tube spacers
- 28 2mm tube spacers
- 16 4mm round beads
- 4 2mm round spacer beads
- 2 crimp beads
- 5mm jump ring
- Clasp

Silver and black necklace
- 21 10mm twisted tube spacers
- 6 18mm oval spacers
- 12 4mm round beads
- 4 2mm round spacer beads
- 2 crimp beads
- 5mm jump ring
- Clasp
- Optional extension: 1 4mm round bead, 2 3mm round beads, 1 head pin, 2 in. (5cm) chain

All necklaces
- Flexible beading wire, .014 or .015
- Chainnose pliers or crimping pliers
- Diagonal wire cutters

Decorative head pin earrings

Decorative head pins add a touch of detail to earrings. Although you can purchase them, you can get the same look with an arrangement of small spacers on a head pin. This is a particularly good idea when you have a large-holed bead that otherwise would slip off the head pin.

Flat-spacer stack: Top a 3mm, a 4mm, and a 5mm with a 12mm round bead **(a)**.

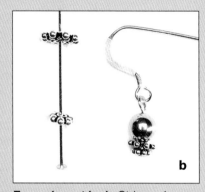

Easy, elegant look: String a 4mm, a 6mm star shape, and a 6mm round bead **(b)**. Finish with a plain loop.

Perfect complement: A 2mm round bead mirrors the earring wire design. Add a 6mm round crystal, and attach with a wrapped loop **(c)**.

Capped crystals bracelets

DESIGN IDEA: Bold bracelets like these deserve a heavy toggle clasp with its own detail. For example, the blue version includes a star-shaped clasp inspired by the star-shaped spacers.

In this design, capping nearly every bead and stacking several spacers between the large cubes really enhances the beauty of the crystals. The lovely star spacers dance and twirl on your wrist.

1. Determine the finished length of your bracelet, add 5 in. (13cm), and cut a piece of beading wire to that length.

2. String two star spacers, a cube, and two star spacers **(a)**.

3. On each side, string a pearl, a bead cap, a bicone, a bead cap, and a pearl **(b)**.

4. Repeat steps 2 and 3 on each side.

5. String two 4mm spacers, a 4mm round, two 4mm spacers, a 4mm round, and two 4mm spacers **(c)**.

6. String a 2mm round, a crimp bead, a 2mm round, and half the clasp. Go back through the beads just strung and a few more. Repeat on the other side **(d)**.

7. Check the fit, and add or remove beads, if necessary. On each end, tighten the wire, and **crimp the crimp bead**. Trim the excess wire.

DESIGN IDEA: The pearls in the green variation are from two different strands, providing several shades of subtle color.

Pattern play bracelets

Spacers can change the personality of beads. Here's a little experiment to see how the same materials can provide different looks. All the bracelets use the same size round beads and flat spacers, strung in different ways. Keep this in mind if you're ever running short of something – sometimes simply rearranging your pattern can help you make the most of your stash.

1. Measure your wrist, add 5 in. (13cm), and cut a piece of flexible beading wire to that length.

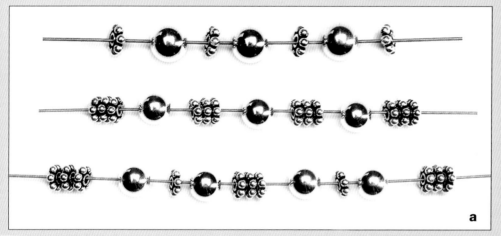

2. String beads and spacers in the pattern of your choice **(a)** until the bracelet is about 1 in. (2.5cm) shorter than you'd like. End with spacers.

3. String a round bead, a crimp bead, a round bead, and half a clasp. Come back through the beads just strung **(b)**.

4. Repeat on the other end, and check the fit. Add or remove any beads, if necessary. **Crimp the crimp beads** and trim the excess wire.

YOU NEED

- 20–30 5mm round beads
- 30–63 4mm flat spacers
- 4 2 or 3mm round beads
- 2 crimp beads
- Toggle clasp or lobster claw clasp and soldered jump ring
- Flexible beading wire, .014 or .015
- Chainnose pliers or crimping pliers
- Diagonal wire cutters

Chapter Six
A review of basics

Caring for your metal jewelry

Metal discolors, or tarnishes, because of exposure to chemicals in the air, including sulfur and oxygen. I've lived in different parts of the country, and I've noticed that my jewelry tarnishes differently in each region. While necklaces hanging out in the open stayed shiny in upstate New York, everything must be out of the air in southeastern Wisconsin. Do you notice tarnish on your favorite silver pieces? You may want to rethink your storage.

Sometimes oxidation is desirable, and there are ways to accelerate the process (see page 65). But most of the time, you want your jewelry to look shiny and new. Wearing your jewelry frequently keeps the tarnish at bay. Storing it in an airtight container, such as a zip-top bag, helps prevent tarnishing too. Anti-tarnish strips – treated paper that neutralizes the sulfur in the air – are a great invention. You can cut them to any size you'd like and store them along with your silver to keep it tarnish-free. Write the date on a corner, and change the strips about twice a year.

Polishing cloths are soft cloths treated with cleaning chemicals. They polish silver, brass, and copper and are easy to use. I keep one in my work area to polish components as I use them – sometimes it's easier to polish a clasp or a flat spacer before attaching it. Fold a cloth over a length of wire and use your pliers to draw the wire through – you'll be amazed at the residue left behind from seemingly shiny wire. Plus, this is a great method for straightening any kinks out of your wire.

You can buy a chemical solution to polish silver and precious-metal jewelry, but it's quite easy to make your own. Add water to a baking soda and salt mixture to make a paste, and scrub the paste onto your jewelry with an old toothbrush. With a little elbow grease, you'll have shiny jewelry the natural way.

Basic jewelry-making techniques

Make a plain loop

1. If you are making a plain loop above a bead, trim the end of the wire to ⅜ in. (1cm) and bend it at a right angle against the bead. (If you are making a plain loop at the end of a wire, grasp the wire with chainnose pliers ⅜ in. from the end and make a right-angle bend.)

2. Grasp the end of the wire with your roundnose pliers ⅛ in. (3mm) from the tips of the jaw. With your index finger, feel to be sure that the wire end is flush with the edge of the pliers. If you feel a stub of wire, you've grasped too far away from the tip, so adjust your pliers. Gently roll the wire until you can't roll comfortably anymore.

3. Reposition the pliers and continue to roll the loop. The tip of the wire should meet the corner of your initial bend, and you should have a perfect, centered wire circle.

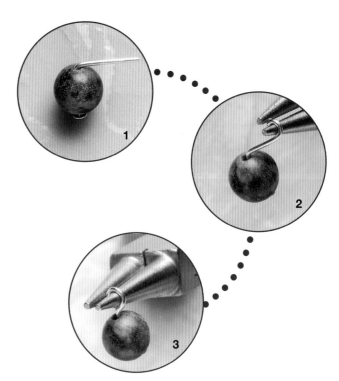

Open and close a plain loop

1. To open a formed loop, grasp it with two pairs of pliers, held parallel to each other. Gently push the loop open by moving one set of pliers forward and the other set backward.

2. Repeat the process in reverse to close the loop. Resist the temptation to unroll the loop. This will overwork the wire and weaken it, and you'll never get a perfectly round loop the second time.

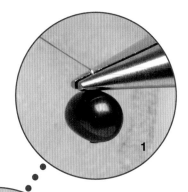

Make a wrapped loop

1. To make a wrapped loop above a bead, trim the wire about 1¼ in. (3.2 cm) above the bead. Grasp the wire with chainnose pliers above the bead, placing the wire about ⅛ in. (3mm) from the tips of the pliers. Fold the wire into a right-angle bend over the pliers. If you're working only with wire (no bead), grasp the wire about 1¼ in. from the end and make a right-angle bend over the pliers.

2. Switch to roundnose pliers and position the jaws in the bend. Bring the end of the wire up and over the top jaw of the pliers and as far down as you can.

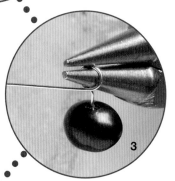

3. Reposition the roundnose pliers so the lower jaw is in the loop. Slide the wire to the same position on the jaw as in step 2. Curve the wire downward around the bottom of the pliers until the tail is at a right angle to the stem. This is called **the first half of a wrapped loop**. At this stage, you can add dangles to the loop or connect the loop to another element, such as a link of chain.

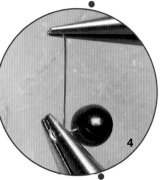

4. To finish the wrapped loop, switch back to chainnose pliers. Position the pliers' jaw across the loop as shown. Use a second pair of pliers – roundnose or chainnose – to grasp the end of the wire and wrap it around the stem. Begin next to the loop and move toward the bead, keeping your wraps as close together as possible.

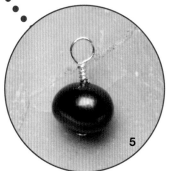

5. One wrap will secure the loop, but several wraps look nicer. Be sure to fill in the entire gap between the loop and the bead so the bead is secure.

Wrap above a top-drilled bead

1. Cut a 3-in. (7.6cm) length of wire, and center a top-drilled bead on the wire. Bend each side upward to form a squared-off U shape. Leave a tiny bit of room for the bead to move – about 1mm.

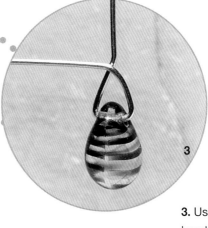

2. Cross the wires into an X above the bead.

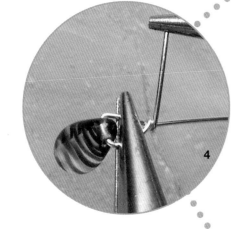

3. Use chainnose pliers to bend one wire straight up and one wire to the side. They'll form a right angle at their intersection.

4. Using two pairs of pliers, wrap the horizontal wire around the vertical wire as in a wrapped loop.

5. Make two or three wraps, and trim the wire.

Open and close a jump ring

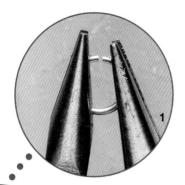

1. Hold the jump ring with two pairs of pliers, as shown.

2. Open the ring by bringing one pair of pliers toward you and pushing the other away.

3. String materials on the open ring as desired. To close, reverse the steps above.

Overhand knot

Make a loop and pass the working ends through it. Pull the ends to tighten.

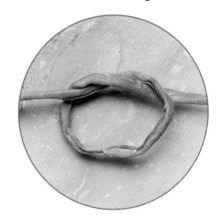

Surgeon's knot

1. Cross the right end over the left and go through the loop. Go through again.

2. Cross the left end over the right and go through. Pull the ends to tighten the knot.

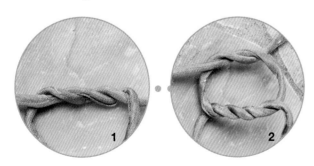

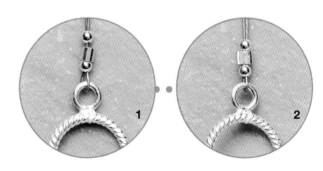

Flatten a crimp

1. String a bead, a crimp, a bead, and a clasp half. Go back through the beads and tighten the wire. Squeeze the crimp with chainnose pliers to flatten.

2. Tug the clasp to be sure the crimp has a solid grip.

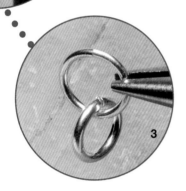

Make a folded crimp

1. Position the crimp tube in the notch closest to the handle of the crimping pliers.

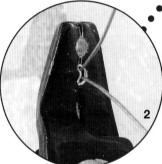

2. Separate the wires and firmly squeeze the crimp.

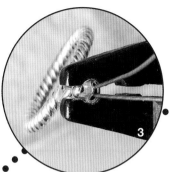

3. Move the crimp to the notch at the pliers' tip and squeeze the crimp bead, folding it in half at the indentation made in step 2.

4. Tug to be sure the crimp is secure.

Attach a fold-over crimp end

1. Apply a dot of GS-Hypo Cement to one end of the cord, and place it in a crimp end. Use chainnose pliers to fold one side of the crimp end over the cord.

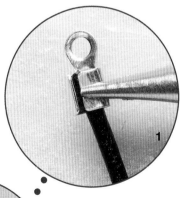

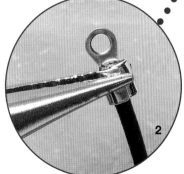

2. Repeat on the second side and squeeze gently.

About the author

Author Karin Buckingham has loved, collected, and crafted jewelry since she was young. As an adult, she became immersed in jewelry professionally as a project designer, writer, and associate editor for *BeadStyle* magazine. At *BeadStyle,* she perfected her jewelry-making skills and found she loved writing about the craft in a way beginners could understand. Since then, she has sold her jewelry designs at art shows, created commissions, and taught classes.

Karin is a lifelong crafter, enjoying other pastimes such as knitting, embroidery, altering clothing, sewing, and cooking. She also is the author of *Altered You!* (Kalmbach Publishing, July 2008). She has a B.A. degree in English from Denison University (Granville, Ohio). Karin now works as an associate editor for Kalmbach Books. She lives in Oconomowoc, Wis., with her husband, Steve; two daughters; and a few pets.

Follow Karin's blog at http://artfulcrafts.blogspot.com

Acknowledgments

If you asked me when I was young what I loved to do, I would have answered, "I like to read, I like to write, and I like to make things." If you asked me what I wanted to do when I grew up, I really didn't have any idea. Now, I get to read, to write, and to make things for a living. I'm not sure if I feel all grown up, but I'm thankful every day that I do what I love.

The whole of my life is far greater than the sum of its parts: part-time editor for Kalmbach Books; part-time jewelry designer and teacher; part-time dog walker and pet tender; part-time housekeeper and errand master; part-time chef and most-time short-order cook; full-time wife, mother, daughter, and sister.

To my family, I am grateful. To my friends, I am thankful. My dog keeps me moving, and my cat reminds me to slow down. My daughters inspire me and provide the perfect balance of unconditional love and unfiltered reality checks. My husband listens patiently to every "what if ..." that I mutter, supports me without question, and brings my visions to life. I love you all.

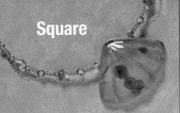

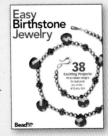
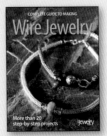
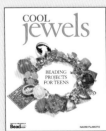